P9-CRM-186

Families Around the World

Written by

Margriet Ruurs

Illustrated by

Jessica Rae Gordon

Kids Can Press

For my whole family, especially Nico and Aidan — M.R.

For my wonderful family and for Jesse, who has been so supportive — J.R.G.

Acknowledgments

Thank you to my editor Valerie Wyatt for guiding me through the labyrinth of language. And a very special thank you to the families from around the world who so generously shared their stories with me. Their lives form the basis of my text. Their generosity in sharing a glimpse of their culture made this book possible.

Canada: Jessica Lu
Mexico: Cindy Albaugh, Larka Tetens and the people of Chumpon
Brazil: Cristiana Jurgensen
England: Rachel Hanna
France: Lucie Bridonneau
Poland: Joanna Podwójna
Israel: the Sharon family
Saudi Arabia: Alkawthar Alshams
Kenya: Rosemary Kinyanjui
Pakistan: Syeda Basarat Kazim, Zaib Husain and family
Mongolia: Eggie Bayandorj, Michele Moller and Jambyn Dashdondog
South Korea: Greg Samborksi and family, Choonghee Ryu and family

First paperback edition 2017

Kids Can Press gratefully acknowledges the financial support of the Government of Ontario, through the Ontario Media Development Corporation; the Ontario Arts Council; the Canada Council for the Arts; and the Government of Canada, through the CBF, for our publishing activity.

Published in Canada and the U.S. by Kids Can Press Ltd.
25 Dockside Drive, Toronto, ON M5A 0B5

Kids Can Press is a Corus Entertainment Inc. company

www.kidscanpress.com

Edited by Valerie Wyatt
Designed by Marie Bartholomew

Printed and bound in Shenzhen, China, in 5/2017 by C & C Offset

CM 14 0 9 8 7 6 5 4 3
CM PA 17 0 9 8 7 6 5 4 3 2 1

Library and Archives Canada Cataloguing in Publication

Ruurs, Margriet, 1952–, author
Families around the world / written by Margriet Ruurs ; illustrated by Jessica Rae Gordon. — First paperback edition 2017.

(Around the world)
ISBN 978-1-894786-57-7 (bound) ISBN 978-1-77138-807-8 (paperback)

1. Families — Juvenile literature. 2. Children — Social life and customs — Juvenile literature.
I. Rae Gordon, Jessica, 1981–, illustrator II. Title.

HQ744.R88 2017 j306.85 C2016-905175-7

Contents

Families Around the World

What can you do to promote world peace?
Go home and love your family!
— Mother Teresa

Families around the world
are different and yet the same.
Some have one child, a mom and a dad.
Others have only one parent or lots of kids.
And some have two moms or two dads.

You may be born into your family, or you may be adopted. Your family may be big or small. Sometimes grandparents, aunts, uncles and cousins all share a family home.

Families love
and support you.
They help you to
discover the world.

No matter which language you speak,
whether you read the Qur'an or the Bible,
pray to Buddha or God or not at all,
live in a house, a hut or a palace,
you are part of a special family!

Come and meet these children and their families.

Sanne
Netherlands
Zofia
Poland
Gilad
Israel
Baatar
Mongolia
Ji Eun
South Korea
Murtaza
& Zaib
Pakistan
Zahra
Saudi Arabia

Ming Chieh's family came from China to live in Vancouver, Canada.

Hello! *Nǐ hǎo!*

My family came to Vancouver
on an airplane. It was a long flight.

My brother and I had to learn
English fast, to help our parents.
Now we speak Mandarin to relatives in
China but make jokes in English at home
and eat lasagna with chopsticks.

Some of my friends at school were born in Canada.
But others came from far away, too.
We swap snacks at lunchtime —
mooncakes for carrot sticks,
rice balls for chocolate chip cookies.

I love to go hiking with
my family in the mountains.
Once, we even spotted a black bear!

Ryan's family runs a cattle ranch in Texas, U.S.A.

Hi!

Sometimes I ride with Dad
on the tractor to check on our cattle.
We have hundreds of cows and steers —
Texas longhorns.

We also have one sheep.
Lambert is all mine,
even though my sister, Rachel,
helps to feed and brush him.
I will enter him in the fall fair.
I hope he wins a ribbon!

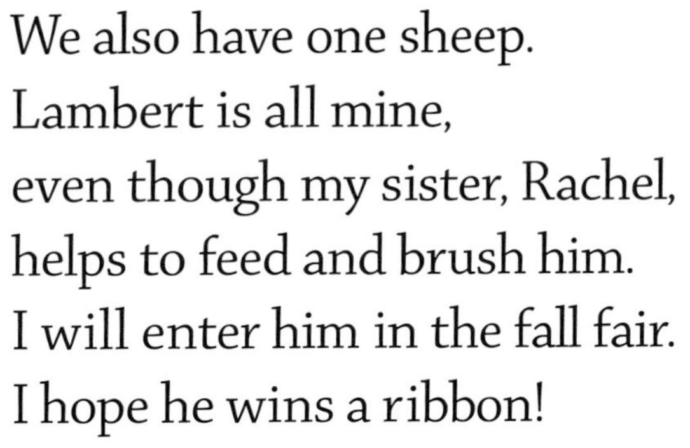

On our farm we grow corn, beets,
potatoes, beans and peas.
I help with weeding
and with eating them, too.

We never go on big trips.
There's too much work on a ranch.
But when my family gathers for dinner,
there's no place in the world I'd rather be.

J-Ch'eel's family lives in a Maya village in Mexico.

Ba'ax ka wa'alik?

The rooster crows.
I roll out of my hammock.
Papá is still snoring,
but *Mamá* is awake.

I gather eggs while *Mamá*
fries *tortillas* for breakfast.
I put on my *huipil* and help my
little brother Carlos get ready for school.
J-Mulix is too little and stays home.

At home we speak Mayan but at
school we learn in Spanish.
I like history best.
Stories about temples and ruins
make me think of our ancestors
who lived in this very same
spot in the jungle.

After school we walk down the
dusty lane through our village.
I hold Carlos's hand.
Friends and cousins join
us along the way.

Cristiana and Antonio's family lives near Rio de Janeiro, Brazil.

Beleza?

On Sunday *Mãe* makes *farofa*.
Pai cooks meat on the grill.
We take turns stirring the beans in a big pot.
The whole family is coming for dinner!

When our grandparents arrive,
we listen to their stories
while we sip *maracujá* juice.

My aunt wants to kiss us,
but we run to greet our cousins.
We play tag and swing from vines.
We hide under the porch, even though
we are wearing our good Sunday clothes.

When we hear the uncles singing,
we know dinner is ready.
I eat so much my belly aches!
Then we dance, laugh and talk
as the stars come out.

Jane's family lives in a small village in England.

Hello!

On days when Mummy and Daddy work, our auntie looks after us. I play in the park while Emmanuel naps in his pram.

After tea and sandwiches, we ride the bus into the city to my ballet lesson.

When Mummy and Daddy come home
from work, we do a puzzle together,
and Dad builds towers with Emmanuel.
Sometimes I talk on the computer with
my grandmother who lives in Nigeria.
I sing her songs that I learned in school.

At bedtime we have a
bath with bubbles.
Then Mummy reads us Bible
stories until we fall asleep.

Sanne's family lives outside Amsterdam in the Netherlands.

Hoi!

I love weekends. No school!
Sometimes our mothers take
my brother, Joris, and me
on the tram into the city.
We visit a museum
or eat *pannekoeken* on a boat.

Other times we ride our bikes
to the petting zoo, to a playground
or just to another village.

Once, we went inside
a windmill to see how it works.
I loved the creaking and
grinding of the wooden gears.

On Sunday we ride our bikes
to the care home where *Oma* lives.
She doesn't remember my name anymore,
but she gives us cookies from an old tin.
I tell her stories that make her smile.

Jean-Luc's family lives in Paris, France.

Bonjour!

Most of the day I am in school.
My teacher is strict, but I like her.

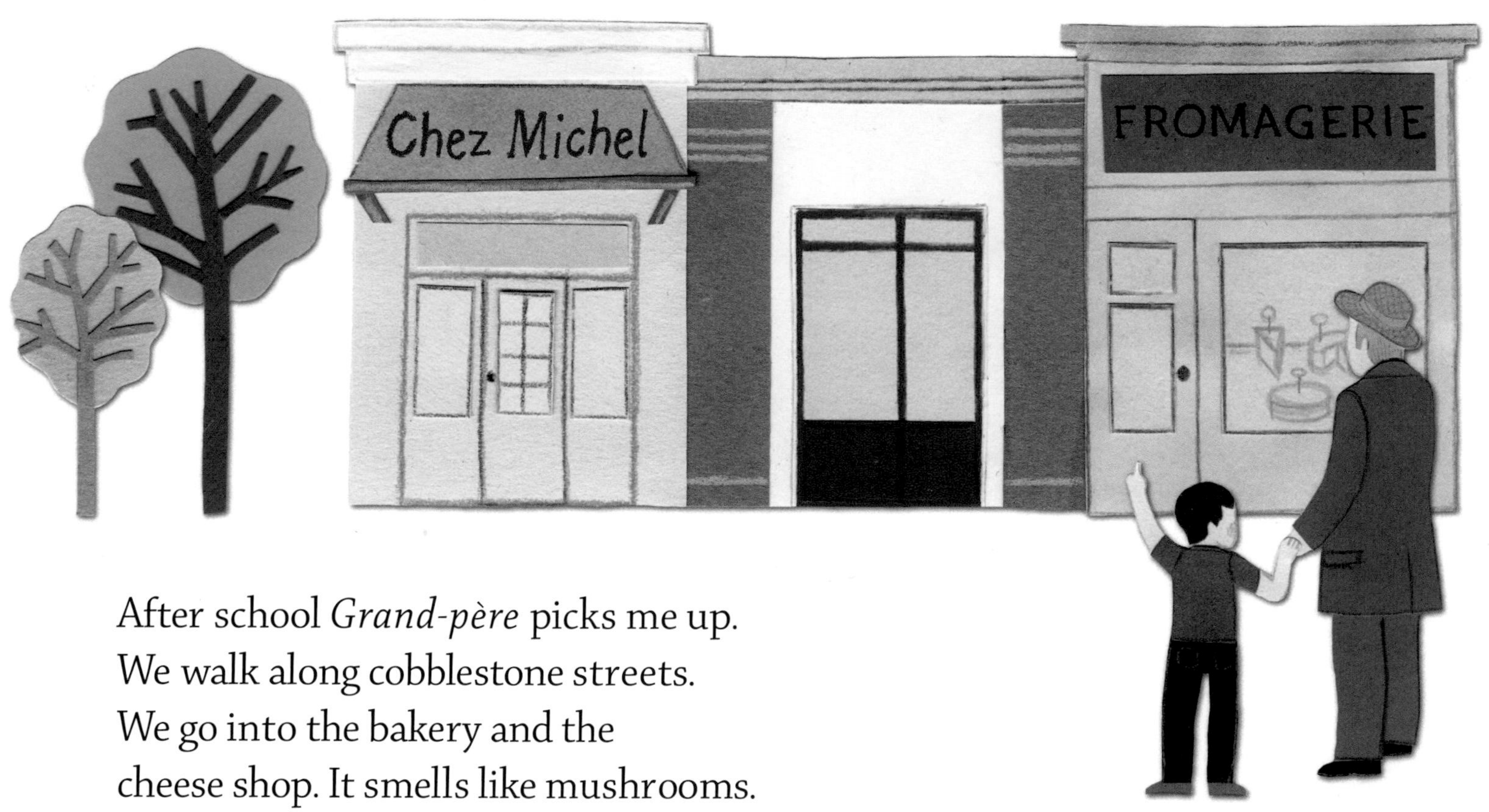

After school *Grand-père* picks me up.
We walk along cobblestone streets.
We go into the bakery and the
cheese shop. It smells like mushrooms.

We buy warm chestnuts to eat in the park.
I play with my friends, and
Grand-père does, too.

Papa arrives at *Grand-père*'s house
as we are making dinner.
We eat around the big wooden table
and talk about our day.
Then *Papa* and I ride
the *Métro* home.

Zofia's family lives in a small town in Poland.

Dzień dobry!

Sunday is my favorite day.
My family walks to church.
The stores are closed.
The town is quiet,
except for church bells ringing out over rooftops.

Back home the house smells good.
Beet soup bubbles on the stove.
I help to cut circles of dough
to make my favorite food — *pierogi*!
Mamusia stuffs them with potatoes and cheese.

Then we all go for a
walk in the woods.
We gather fall leaves
and mushrooms.
My nose turns red from the cold.

In the evening *Tata* listens to classical music.
Mamusia knits a warm sweater.
My brother, Wiktor, and I play video games
until our parents remember it is bedtime!

Gilad's family lives on a *kibbutz* in Israel.

Shalom!

Our *kibbutz* is like a village
where everyone works together.
We have our own house,
but we all eat
in one big dining room.

After school my friends and I walk around
the *kibbutz*, singing songs and laughing.
We eat orange rinds with coconut
and play tag.

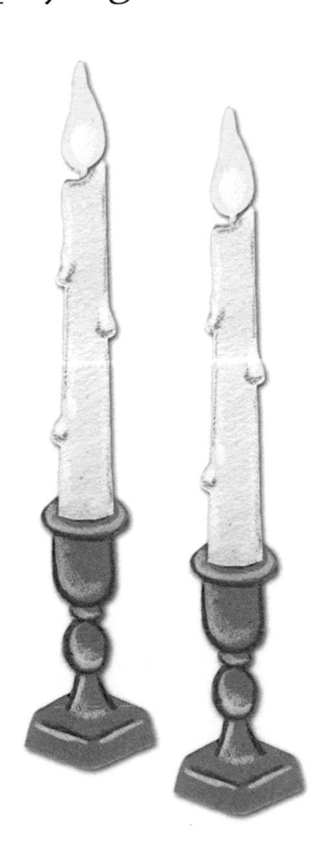

Every Friday night we have *Shabbat*.
We gather just before sunset
to light candles and sing songs.

It makes me feel good
to be part of this big family.

Zahra's family lives in an old city in Saudi Arabia.

Assalamu Alaikum!

Our family wakes before sunrise to pray,
to get ready for a new day.
Ummi kisses us goodbye
and wishes us well at school.
We hurry off — school
starts at 6:30 a.m.

I like computer class and
memorizing verses from the Qur'an.
My favorite thing is to
read stories about other countries.
But I don't like homework!

On Thursday night our weekend
starts with a big family meal.
Then my cousins and I play
hide-and-seek and soccer in the backyard.

At sunset we do our prayers,
as we do five times a day.
When I go to sleep I dream of
traveling the world one day.

Nkoitoi's family lives in a Maasai village in Kenya.

Sopa!

The sun is not up yet, but I am.
The rooster crowed me awake.
I tiptoe outside to fetch water for tea.
Once the sun rises,
I gather firewood,
so we can cook *ugali* for lunch.

I look after our family goat.
Her kids jump for joy and nearly
butt the water jug out of my hands.

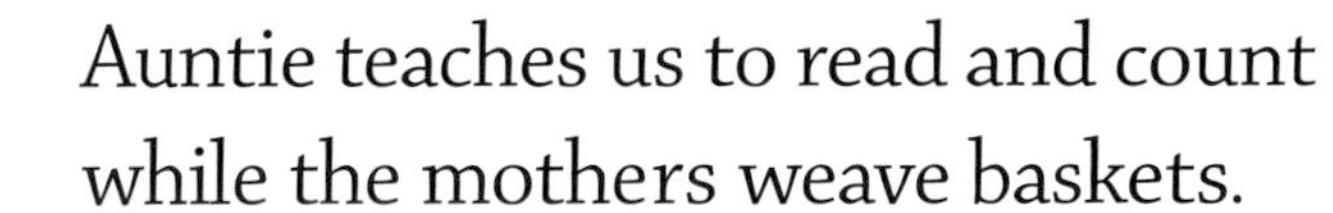

Auntie teaches us to read and count
while the mothers weave baskets.

At night I listen to stories the elders tell.
They say that the times are changing,
but I hope some things will stay the same.

Murtaza, Zaib and their family live in Lahore, Pakistan.

Assalamu Alaikum!

Ammi wakes us early every morning to get ready for school.

After school our father picks us up.
Today he has a surprise.
We ride through busy traffic.
Are we going to a soccer match?
To the museum?

No! *Abba* drives us
to the village where he was born.
He shows us where he lived
and went to school.
We see the roses Grandfather planted
when *Abba* was a boy.

Back home we have lots to tell our family.
Then we read from the Qur'an together,
and our parents tuck us into bed.
Tomorrow, *Inshallah,* will bring new adventures.

Baatar is part of a nomadic family in the Gobi Desert of Mongolia.

Sain bain uu!

My family lives in a *ger*, a round tent. On the stove, there is always mutton soup and hot water to make salty tea.

I have many chores.
I gather camel dung patties to burn
in the stove, and I feed the baby goats.
When I'm done, I ride my horse and pretend
to be Genghis Khan, our Mongolian hero.

At the end of summer, it is time to move.
We load the camels with our folded *ger*
and everything we own.
We ride across the desert to a
new place to spend the winter.

I listen to my father play the horse-head fiddle
and to *Eej*, who is throat singing.
No matter where we are,
our home is warm and cozy.

Ji Eun's family lives in Seoul, South Korea.

Anyang ha say yo!

After a breakfast of rice and soup,
Uhm-ma and *Apba* hurry off to work.
My grandmother walks me to school.
I bow to my teacher, then slide into my desk.

After school I go to *hogwon*,
a special homework class.
Sometimes there are tests
to make sure we are learning lots.
I also practice the piano.

It is dark when my grandmother picks me up.
We meet my parents at the shopping center.
We eat *kimbap* and soybeans
and buy a new *hanbok* for me.

At home I try on my *hanbok*.
My grandmother claps as I perform a dance.
She says I am a better dancer than anyone on TV!

Your Family

Families come in
all shapes and sizes.
What is your family like?

Do your grandparents live
in the same house as you do,
like Murtaza and Zaib's
grandparents in Pakistan?

Did your family move to another country like
Ming Chieh, who came to Canada from China?
Do your grandparents speak a
different language than you do?

Do you have more than one mom
like Sanne in the Netherlands
or only one parent like
Jean-Luc in France?

Do you have lots of aunts, uncles and
cousins who visit on special days?

It doesn't matter where in the world you live —
in a castle or under a palm leaf roof.
Families around the world
have the same hopes and dreams!

A Note for Parents and Teachers

The stories in this book are all based on real families, many of whom have become my friends in the process of writing this book. One thing became very clear to me as I talked to them: people have very similar hopes and dreams for their children, no matter where they live. I hope that awareness of other cultures and other people's experiences will guide us toward a better understanding of the world around us.

The following activities are aimed at enriching children's reading experience. Use them as is or tailor them to fit into your daily life. Even more ideas can be found on my website: www.margrietruurs.com

Pinpointing on the Map

Using a globe or atlas, show children where they live, then locate each of the countries in the book. The countries are arranged west to east, starting with Canada. By moving around the globe as you work your way through the countries, you can take children on a trip around the world.

Get the Details

To compile the information in this book, I interviewed families from around the world. Ask children to interview a family member. Help them compile questions about the relative's childhood and memories of other family members.

Make a Passport

Following the steps below, turn a piece of paper into a pocket-size passport. Decorate it to look like a passport and add postage stamps from the countries you "visit." Or use potato stamps.

1. Start with a sheet of paper.

2. Fold in half shortwise.

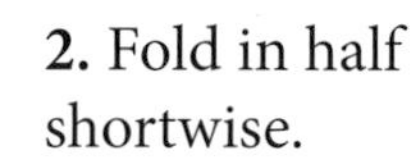

3. Fold back one edge to the middle fold.

4. Fold back the other edge to the middle fold.

5. Unfold the sheet, then fold longwise.

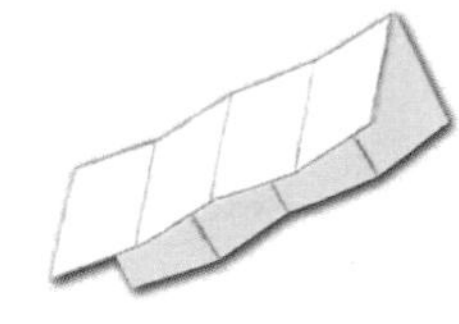

6. Refold shortwise, then use scissors to cut along the line marked here in red.

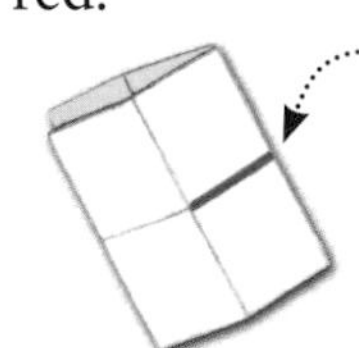

7. Refold longwise. Holding each end, push toward the middle to open up where you made the cut.

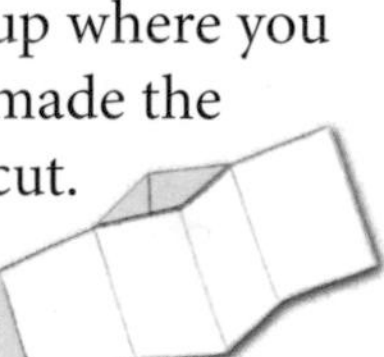

8. Push all the way in.

9. Fold the left edge over to create the cover. Now it is a tiny passport.

Hello!

As you can see in this book, there are many ways of saying "hello" around the world. Ming Chieh, who now lives in Canada, would have said "*Nǐ hǎo!*" in China, which translates to "Are you well?" The glossary on page 40 gives pronunciation guides. Ask children to say "hello" in the other languages in the book. Ask what other languages they know. What is "hello" in the language of their ancestry?

On a large sheet of paper, trace around each child and cut out the life-size paper child. Color in clothing from their cultural backgrounds and cut out large speech bubbles with the word for "hello" in their language. These paper figures can decorate a house, classroom, school hallway or entrance.

Read Closely

There are many differences among the families in this book — but also many similarities.

- Some children in the book help with chores. Ask children to find an example. Ask what chores *they* do around their house.
- Some children in the book play sports. Ask children in which countries the children play soccer. Discuss *their* favorite sports.
- Ask children to draw a picture of what a house might look like in South Korea, Mongolia and Kenya. Discuss how each house is different.

Food

Some children in the book mention their favorite foods. Ask children to find three examples. Have they ever tried any of the foods? What is *their* favorite food?

Family Tree

Some families in this book have one child, others have many. Families may also include grandparents, aunts and uncles. To talk about families, help children draw family trees. In which country or culture does their family tree have roots?

Traveling the World

Using a map of the world or globe, ask children to point to any country in which they know someone or have visited.

Contact me through my website to find a pen pal or to exchange a bookmark with someone in another country.

Ask children where they would go if they could travel to any country in the book. Why?

Write Around the World

Which child in the book lives in a *ger*? What would it be like to live in a *ger*? Tell a story together. Write it down and have the child or children illustrate it.

Ask children to write an acrostic poem about their families, grandmothers or grandfathers.

F araway cousins

A unts and uncles

M y mom and dad

I like my whole family

L ove my baby sister

Y our family is special, too!

Glossary

Pages 8–9, Canada
Nĭ hăo (nee-HOW): Hello. Are you well?

Pages 12–13, Mexico (Maya)
Ba'ax ka wa'alik (BAH-ah-shko-WAH-ah-LEEK): Hello
Papá: Father
Mamá: Mother
tortillas: round flatbreads
huipil: traditional embroidered shirt or dress

Pages 14–15, Brazil
Beleza (bay-LAY-zch): Hello. All good?
Mãe: Mother
farofa: raw manioc flour toasted with butter, salt, spices and smoked meats
Pai: Father
maracujá: passion fruit

Pages 18–19, Netherlands
Hoi (hoy): Hello
pannekoeken: thin, rolled-up pancakes with syrup
Oma: Grandmother

Pages 20–21, France
Bonjour (bhon-ZJOOR): Hello. Good day.
Grand-père: Grandfather
Papa: Father
Métro: subway system

Pages 22–23, Poland
Dzień dobry (GIN-doh-bree): Hello
pierogi: dough pockets filled with cottage cheese and potatoes
Mamusia: Mother
Tata: Father

Pages 24–25, Israel
Shalom (shah-LOHM): Hello. Peace.
kibbutz: a community where many families live and work together
Shabbat: a weekly day of rest and a time to worship

Pages 26–27, Saudi Arabia
Assalamu Alaikum (ah-sala-moo-a-LIKE-oom): Peace be with you
Ummi: Mother
Qur'an: the holy book of Islam

Pages 28–29, Kenya
Sopa (SOH-pah): Hello
ugali: a mixture of maize flour and water

Pages 30–31, Pakistan
Assalamu Alaikum (ah-sala-moo-a-LIKE-oom): Peace be with you
Ammi: Mother
Abba: Father
Qur'an: the holy book of Islam
Inshallah: God willing. Let us hope it will happen.

Pages 32–33, Mongolia
Sain bain uu (sein-BAH-noo): Hello. How are you?
ger: traditional, round tent
Eej: Mother

Pages 34–35, South Korea
Anyang ha say yo (an-YONG-ha-say-yo): How are you?
Uhm-ma: Mother
Apba: Father
hogwon: after-school academy
kimbap: popular dish of rice rolled in seaweed
hanbok: traditional dress